Noddy and the Magic Bagpipes

HarperCollins *Children's Books*

It was a chilly day in Toyland…

Big-Ears and Noddy were playing a game in Toadstool House. Noddy was puzzling over his next move, when Big-Ears wanted a warm rug.

Noddy leaped up. “I’ll get it!” he said.

BLARRRRP!

"Agghh!" gasped Noddy. "There's a monster in your cupboard, Big-Ears!"

Big-Ears strode towards the cupboard.

"Ooooh! Be careful, Big-Ears," Noddy warned him. "It sounds very angry."

Big-Ears reached into the cupboard.

BLARRRRP!

Noddy jumped back in horror.

Big-Ears chuckled. "Don't be scared, Noddy," he said. "That's not a monster. That's my bagpipes. I can play music on them. Listen."

Big-Ears took a big, deep breath and blew into the bagpipes. His fingers danced over the holes and the bagpipes let out a loud *wagh-wagh-wagh* tune.

"What a wonderful sound!" sighed Noddy, dreamily. How magical it would be if *he* could play the bagpipes!

"Will you teach me to play?" Noddy asked.

"It takes a lot of time and practice to play the bagpipes, Noddy," Big-Ears warned.

"But I really want to learn. Please teach me, Big-Ears," Noddy begged.

Big-Ears looked serious. "These are special bagpipes, Noddy," he said. "They need a lot of care. And you must practise. You have to play them every day."

"Yes, yes, I'll do it," agreed Noddy. "I'll work really hard, Big-Ears, I promise."

Big-Ears smiled as they got ready for Noddy's first lesson.

"Let's start now," whooped Noddy.

"I'll teach you a simple tune," said Big-Ears. "Then you must practise it every single day. Understand?"

"Yes, Big-Ears," said Noddy, eagerly. "I'll practise first thing, every day."

Next morning, Noddy leaped out of bed. He wrestled the bagpipes into position, took a big, deep breath and blew.

BLARRRPP-RRRNNNNN-SSSSSHHH!

"That didn't sound anything like the tune Big-Ears played," grumbled Noddy. "I'll try again."

And he took another big, deep breath.

But just as Noddy was about to blow into the pipes, he saw his yellow kite leaning against the wall.

"There's a perfect breeze today. I think I'll fly my kite," said Noddy, throwing the bagpipes on to the chair. "I can always practise tomorrow."

Next morning, Noddy was just about to start practising, when he heard Mr Sparks' voice.

"Hey, Noddy! Do you want to come fishing?"

"Sorry! I'm rather busy," Noddy called down.

Then he saw Mr Sparks' fishing rod.

"I can always practise the bagpipes tomorrow," Noddy said to himself.

And again, he dropped them on the chair.

The following morning, Noddy said to himself, "Today, I won't let anything stop me from practising."

And he leaped out of bed and reached for the bagpipes. But the wonderful bagpipes had gone!

Noddy searched everywhere for them.

"Oh dear, Big-Ears *will* be upset!" he cried.

Down at his garage, Mr Sparks was busy working on a car.

The bagpipes crept up quietly beside him and... BLARRRP!

"Yahhhhh!" Mr Sparks jumped back and clunked his head. "What was THAT?" he wondered, looking up and down the empty street.

In the square, Dinah Doll was putting the last building block on a tower.

"There," she said, happily. "Now everyone will notice my stall."

BLARRRP! The cheeky bagpipes gave poor Dinah such a fright, she tumbled off her ladder.

"Whoaaaahh!" she yelled as she fell in a shower of blocks.

Dinah Doll and Mr Sparks were telling Mr Plod what had happened, when Noddy ran up to them.

"Mr Plod, there's been a bagpipes robbery!"

"Bagpipes, eh?" said Mr Plod. "I've just heard about a mysterious musical instrument on the loose in Toy Town."

BLARRRP! BLARRRP! BLARRRP!

"Listen!" cried Noddy. "It's the bagpipes."

Just at that moment, there was a clattering sound and Noddy and his friends looked round. But all they saw was a blur of tartan as the bagpipes dashed past.

WHEEEET! Mr Plod blew his whistle.

"Stop in the name of Plod!" he ordered, but the bagpipes took no notice and ran on, whining and wailing.

Mr Plod chased the bagpipes all around the town, trying to grab them. Noddy, Mr Sparks and Dinah watched, amazed.

Nimbly, the bagpipes leaped out of Mr Plod's reach and sped away.

"Oooof," he gasped.

"Looks like Mr Plod needs our help," said Dinah.

But the cheeky bagpipes leaped up at Dinah and Mr Sparks, and then clattered away as they tumbled over backwards.

"Ouch!" they both cried.

"Come back here, you!" shouted Noddy.

But the bagpipes took no notice.

Noddy ran round and round after the bagpipes, until he was dizzy.

"Now where has that pesky thing gone?" he wondered. BLAARRRP!

Noddy looked up. Perched on a branch were the bagpipes. He grabbed one of the dangling pipes and pulled.

"Got you!" he yelled.

Noddy held on tight, but the bagpipes began to grow bigger and bigger.

Suddenly, they let out a loud BLARRP! and took off. They were flying!

"Help! Help!" Noddy shouted, clinging on to the whooshing bagpipes.

As Noddy swooped past, Mr Plod grabbed hold of his feet. But Mr Plod was swept up into the air as well!

"Aghhh!" he gasped.

Then Mr Sparks grabbed on to Mr Plod's legs and Dinah grabbed Mr Sparks' legs.

But the clever bagpipes swooped down under a park bench – and zoomed out the other side without them.

That night, the bagpipes' non-stop wailing kept the whole of Toy Town awake.

Noddy gave up trying to sleep.

"I have to catch those bagpipes," he groaned.

Suddenly, Noddy heard a loud knocking on his door. Perhaps it was the bagpipes? He jumped out of bed.

"Big-Ears!" cried Noddy, as he opened the door.

"You didn't practise, did you?" said Big-Ears, crossly. "I warned you those bagpipes had to be played every day."

"I'm sorry, Big-Ears. I *did* mean to," Noddy said sadly.

He looked so upset that Big-Ears sighed, "Don't worry, Noddy. I just get grumpy when I'm tired."

"But why are the bagpipes running around screeching?" asked Noddy. "And keeping us all awake?"

"Magic," explained Big-Ears. "These bagpipes get restless if they're not played every day. They just want to make music – but they need help… which gives me an idea, Noddy!"

"A-one, a-two, a-three," said Big-Ears to his brand new band in Toy Town park.

BUZZ-BUZZ-BUZZ went Dinah on the kazoo.

WHEET-WHEET went Mr Plod on his whistle.

BOOM-BOOM went Mr Sparks on an oil drum.

And Noddy sang:

The best thing about this simple song
Is that anyone can play along...

The bagpipes watched the band. Then they leaped on to Noddy's chair.

Scooping them on to his lap, Noddy took a big, deep breath and blew. *Wagh-wagh-wagh…*

The bagpipes were happy now that they were making music in a real band.

And Noddy played every note perfectly.

"Wonderful!" said Big-Ears. "Our music has tamed the bagpipes!"

"But I think you ought to give them back to Big-Ears for safe-keeping, Noddy," said Mr Sparks.

"Yes," said Noddy. "You'd better have the bagpipes, Big-Ears. I might not practise every day!"

"OK, Noddy," said Big-Ears, smiling. "But first, let's play our tune just one more time."

"Right!" said Noddy, and took a big, deep breath.

And the new Toy Town band gave one last wonderful performance.

The best thing about this simple song
Is that anyone can play along.
Listen to the tune, and feel the beat,
Then clap your hands and stamp your feet!

First published in Great Britain by HarperCollins Publishers Ltd in 2003

This edition published by HarperCollins Children's Books in Great Britain in 2005.
HarperCollins Children's Books is a division of HarperCollins Publishers Ltd.

For further information on Noddy please contact www.NODDY.com

A CIP catalogue for this title is available from the British Library.

Visit our website at: www.harpercollinschildrensbooks.co.uk

Printed and bound by Printing Express Ltd, Hong Kong

Noddy Goes Shopping

HarperCollins *Children's Books*

It was a peaceful morning in Toy Town...

PARP! PARP! The startled folk of Toy Town looked up as Noddy's car hurtled through the streets.

"We made it!" gasped Mrs Skittle as the car screeched to a halt at the station.

"Now, Noddy," she said. "How much do I owe you?"

Noddy wasn't sure.

"Um, did I say two children count as one grown up, or…"

"Noddy!" cried Mrs Skittle. "I don't have time for this. Here! Keep the change." And she dropped a heap of coins into his hand.

"Oh!" cried Noddy. "What a lot of money!"

Noddy jumped into his car and zoomed across town to Big-Ears' house.

"Hello, Big-Ears!" cried Noddy, running up the stairs. "I've just earned loads of money. We could go out and spend it on… oh!"

He stopped in surprise.

Big-Ears was still in bed!

"Big-Ears! It's the middle of the morning and you're still asleep!" said Noddy.

"I wish I *was* asleep," Big-Ears yawned, loudly. "That's the problem. I just can't seem to get to sleep at all."

"Then why don't you go to bed early?" suggested Noddy.

"I can't get to sleep!" said Big-Ears, crossly. "If I weren't so tired, I'd go into town to buy the things I need to make a sleeping charm."

"*I'll* go for you!" cried Noddy.

"That's very kind," said Big-Ears. "Now, listen: I'll need a small cloth bag to hold everything."

"Small cloth bag," repeated Noddy. "Got it."

"A bunch of night-blooming flowers to make me feel sleepy."

"OK," said Noddy. "What else?"

Big-Ears thought hard. "A small black stone, to make my eyes feel heavy."

"Right," said Noddy. "Small black stone."

"And a few little white balls of cotton wool to use as ear plugs. Oh, yes, and a torch, to remind me of the calming moonlight."

"You must remember all the things," said Big-Ears. "If you forget just one of them, the charm won't work."

"Don't worry, Big-Ears!" said Noddy.

Big-Ears yawned. "And I also need a toy saw," he said. "It'll get me snoring."

"Six things," said Noddy, as he headed for the door. "I'll remember all of them!"

Big-Ears checked the time. "Noddy should be back in about half an hour."

And he settled back to wait.

One hour and forty-five minutes later, Noddy had still not come back.

"Where on earth *is* Noddy?" yawned Big-Ears. "He should be back by now."

The clock ticked away.

But still Noddy did not come back. Big-Ears grew more and more worried.

Just then, he heard the front door open, and the sound of eager footsteps coming up the stairs.

"I'm back!" cried Noddy, bursting into the room.

"What took you so long?" asked Big-Ears.

"Sorry," said Noddy, dumping a large box on the floor. "It just took a while to get all six things."

“Here’s the cloth bag,” said Noddy,
pulling a large sack out of the box.

Big-Ears peered into it.

“I can’t see any little bag.
Are you sure it’s in here?”

"It's not *in* the sack," laughed Noddy. "It *is* the sack!"

"Noddy," groaned Big-Ears, "I said a *small* bag."

"Oops!" said Noddy. "Does it matter? Surely, the bigger the better?"

Big-Ears sighed.

"What about the ear plugs?" asked Big-Ears.

Noddy handed Big-Ears some hard white balls.

"Oh, no! Not golf balls!" wailed Big-Ears. "I said *cotton wool* balls."

Noddy shrugged. "All I could remember was white balls. Sorry!"

Big-Ears shook his head. "Well, Noddy… did you remember the small black stone?"

Noddy pulled a big, grey rock out of the box.

"Honestly, Noddy," frowned Big-Ears. "I said a small black stone. This is big and grey!"

"Oh, dear. I forgot about the size," said Noddy, "but I didn't forget the colour!"

He pulled out a black pencil and started scribbling on the rock.

"Have you remembered *anything* properly?" moaned Big-Ears.

Noddy put his hand back into the box.

"What is that for?" asked Big-Ears, crossly.

"A car headlight for your moonlight, silly!" said Noddy. "Now *you* don't remember!"

"No, no, no, no, *no*!" cried Big-Ears. "I said a *torch*, not a *headlight*."

"Won't a headlight do?" asked Noddy.

"Well, at least I remembered the tool to make you snore!" said Noddy.

Big-Ears couldn't believe Noddy had been so silly. "I said *saw*, Noddy. Not *spanner*."

"Oh dear! What a bad memory I have," said Noddy. "But look, you could try this..." And he put the spanner on his nose.

Big-Ears pulled the spanner off Noddy's nose.

"I expect you've muddled up the flowers as well," sighed Big-Ears.

Noddy put his hand into the box and pulled out a bunch of dead weeds.

"Wrong!" groaned Big-Ears. "Just like everything else!"

“Noddy,” Big-Ears said sadly, “you didn’t remember one single thing.”

Noddy hung his head.

“I’m really sorry, Big-Ears,” he said. “I just don’t have a very good memory.”

Big-Ears smiled. “No, you don’t. But you do have a good forgetery!”

Noddy sighed in relief. “Thank goodness you’re not really cross, Big-Ears. I tried my best, truly I did.”

“I know,” said Big-Ears. “But if you need to remember something, write it down.”

“What a good idea!” whooped Noddy, happily.

Big-Ears quickly wrote out a shopping list.

"Thanks," said Noddy. "Now I'll remember everything!" And he picked up the box and rushed downstairs.

Seconds later, he was back.

"Err… I forgot the list, Big-Ears," he said, as he grabbed it.

Big-Ears grinned as he shuffled back to bed.

"That boy… Oops!" Big-Ears' foot slipped on a golf ball.

BOING! He hit the bed and then bounced up to the ceiling. THWACK! Down he came with a mighty THUD! Big-Ears was out cold!

A little while later, Noddy came back.

"I managed to get everything on the list!" he called. "Now you can get some sleep, Big-Ears. … oh!"

He stopped, staring in astonishment.

"Zzzz-zzzz-zzzz." Big-Ears was fast asleep, snoring loudly. He looked very comfortable.

Noddy crept over to the bed.

"Maybe you didn't need the sleeping charm after all," he whispered.

"Good night!" said Noddy, and he pulled the bedcovers gently over Big-Ears and tiptoed out.

"Zzzzzzzzzzzzzz..."

First published in Great Britain by HarperCollins Publishers Ltd in 2003

This edition published by HarperCollins Children's Books in Great Britain in 2005.
HarperCollins Children's Books is a division of HarperCollins Publishers Ltd.

For further information on Noddy please contact www.NODDY.com

A CIP catalogue for this title is available from the British Library.

Visit our website at: www.harpercollinschildrensbooks.co.uk

Printed and bound by Printing Express Ltd, Hong Kong

make way for NODDY™

Do-It-Yourself Noddy
ISBN 0 00 712241 1

Noddy Goes Shopping
ISBN 0 00 712242 X

Collect them all!

Hold on to your Hat, Noddy
ISBN 0 00 712243 8

The Magic Powder
ISBN 0 00 715101 2

Noddy and the Magic Bagpipes
ISBN 0 00 712366 3

Noddy and the New Taxi
ISBN 0 00 712239 X

Bounce Alert in Toy Town
ISBN 0 00 715103 9

A Bike for Big-Ears
ISBN 0 00 715105 5

Noddy's Perfect Gift
ISBN 0 00 712365 5

Noddy's Special Treat
ISBN 0 00 712362 0

Noddy on the Move
ISBN 0 00 715678 2

Noddy the Rainbow Chaser
ISBN 0 00 715677 4

And send off for your free Noddy poster (rrp £3.99).
Simply collect 4 tokens and complete the coupon below.

TOKEN

Name: ______________________________

Address: ______________________________

____

____

e-mail: ______________________________

❑ Tick here if you do not wish to receive further information about children's books.

Send coupon to: **Noddy Poster Offer, PO Box 142, Horsham, RH13 5FJ**

Terms and conditions: proof of sending cannot be considered proof of receipt. Not redeemable for cash. 28 days delivery. Offer open to UK residents only.

Make Way for Noddy videos (**Noddy and the New Taxi** and **Hold on to your Hat, Noddy**) now available at all good retailers

UNIVERSAL